INDIA'S F
VENTILATOR

Dark Secrets of Indian Hospitality Industry & Strategies for Driving Profitable Success

by
ARCHIT SINGHAL

V&S PUBLISHERS

Published by:

V&S PUBLISHERS

F-2/16, Ansari road, Daryaganj, New Delhi-110002
☎ 23240026, 23240027 • *Fax:* 011-23240028
✉ info@vspublishers.com • ⊕ www.vspublishers.com

 Online Brandstore: amazon.in/vspublishers

Regional Office : Hyderabad
5-1-707/1, Brij Bhawan (Beside Central Bank of India Lane)
Bank Street, Koti, Hyderabad - 500 095
☎ 040-24737290
✉ vspublishershyd@gmail.com

Follow us on:

BUY OUR BOOKS FROM: AMAZON FLIPKART

© Copyright: Author
ISBN 978-81-978303-7-2
New Edition

Printed at : Param Offsetters, Okhla, New Delhi–110020

Contents

For my *Mom*, who will
always be my guiding light

For my *Dad*, my backbone

For my *Wife*, my shadow

For my *Daughter*, whose joy is my life

For all the time, I never give up!

Preface

This book is a summation of my 10-year experience operating in the food and beverage industry and how the industry has evolved over the last decade, accompanied by personal experiences. It explores how one of the largest employers of unorganized labor is undergoing a period of stagnant growth, where wealth is being accumulated in an uneven manner. The hospitality industry remains one of the most underpaid and selfish sectors, where the majority of employees have experienced minimal salary growth amidst an environment of increasing work hours and rising inflation. Despite being an avid reader and book collector, I have yet to find a single book in any bookstore or library that addresses the current affairs of this industry comprehensively.

India is at the forefront of rising disposable incomes, and the middle class is increasingly venturing out and developing a palate for global cuisines. However, without a proper infrastructure of hotel management colleges and updated courses, students graduating from hotel management colleges struggle to cope with the evolving demands and trends of the hospitality industry. A significant portion of students tend to join the lower echelons of the hotel industry or change their profession altogether after failing to receive the respect they anticipated from their intellectual pursuits. Most current employees working in the hospitality sector remain unskilled, with many migrating from smaller towns to urban areas in hopes of securing a stable career.

This book serves as a reality check, shedding light on the looming issues within our vibrant and ever-growing industry. It is a valuable resource for anyone planning or starting a career in the F&B industry or for those currently working or associated with the sector, offering insights and highlighting gaps to help individuals reach their full potential. This work is born out of frustration over long-standing issues that have been consistently ignored by industry players, despite my efforts to bring them to the forefront. There is a lack of clear leadership guiding the industry, as everyone is engaged in a battle for survival. A range of issues will be highlighted across various sectors involved in food and beverages. In the first 18 chapters, I will discuss different gaps in the F&B sector that are affecting the industry on a larger scale and suggest solutions at the end of each chapter to help us evolve into one of the most respected and profitable industries.

There is an urgent need for reforms in our industry, as a significant portion of the workforce is enduring difficult times, which will soon take a toll on their mental and physical well-being. Every individual working in the service industry is engaged in a demanding job that requires great resilience and discipline on a daily basis. I salute these warriors. This book is a plea for everyone to be the change they wish to see, ultimately benefiting all stakeholders in the long run.

1

Evolution of Beverages

"Beverages have to be created. And they're created by looking at what trend is in, say, the fashion industry-what color's hot right now"
– Howard Schultz, CEO, Starbucks

Coming from a family background where travel has been ingrained in our DNA, I have religiously followed in my parents' footsteps of extensive traveling during every available break since passing out of school. Food and beverages had already piqued my interest, I believe the selfless service to others and the vast exposure to strangers and new people caught my attention, unlike the investment banking industry, where most of the time is spent working on valuations in Excel, only to be told by the boss to work around a predetermined number.

I realized that, being a Libra with a touch of humor, I was destined for this industry. However, I remained sharp with mathematics from my college days. During my MBA, my college mates nicknamed me "Chidu" due to the celebrated Finance Minister at the time, P. Chidambaram. I recognized that I had an affinity for numbers and taught countless friends and hostel mates about finance.

Hailing from Delhi, my days in Mumbai were numbered and lonely, with most of my time spent studying in the library playing with financial figures, and reading annual reports, which slowly became a hobby. I was quick to analyze and draw conclusions from certain numbers. I always thought that great brands with businesses were built on strong cash flow or proper financial management.

Coming from a business family. I always wanted to be an entrepreneur, I realized that a job was merely a means to learn at the company's expense; learning took precedence over money for me. I was quick to read biographies and learn about great companies or brands, and realized that most of the paths taken were quite common. Many a times, I feel that success is simple if the focus is correct with proper discipline is applied. However, in 2015, when I realized that the investment role had entirely and mentally exhausted my energy and focus, I had to move on.

I started looking at sector as an option and stumbled upon a short assignment to record pre-recorded videos for CFA exam preparation in Bangalore for 10 days. During my visit to Bangalore, I realized that the beverage industry was extremely underdeveloped compared to Western countries and even the food sector, given that beverages and food contribute equally or more to the hospitality industry. The beverage industry was at a nascent stage, and the consumer knowledge was limited to basic drinks. Bangalore, with its well informed and well-traveled audience, understood the tasting palate for drinks.

I realized there were many gaps that required to be worked upon. Thereafter, I started utilizing my financial acumen to identify trends, concepts, and understand pain points in the beverage industry, specifically in the alcohol space. I worked with multiple liquor companies and created a few intellectual properties focused on festivals and masterclasses. I networked with multiple restaurants, bar owners and the bartending community. It seemed that most of the leading players were passionate about their work, and the owners were doing well financially to grow their businesses. Most of my interactions were with the top tier of the industry.

Slowly, over time, I started talking and doing honest work with the bartending industry. However, I realized we were pursuing an opaque goal without a proper direction. Everyone was complaining about one another, and no one was happy in each other's company. The owners had a strong background or family business, which never compelled them to work with the team at the ground level to understand the real issues. All the management of bars or restaurants was handed over to managers, and owners were just like any other guests visiting their brands.

I started talking to many people at the ground level about the issues and hosted a few competitions as part of my intellectual property, Cocktail Week, which I founded in 2015. Later, it was attempted to be copied by many industry leaders, thanks to the weak trademark laws in our country.

Coming back to the issues, the industry had passionate people, and with a little pampering coupled with appreciation, they excelled. Creating platforms for talent was sorely lacking in industry, where most networking and industry events revolved around appreciating leaders and owners. The majority of employees remained ignored and depressed, unable to get off from their miserable situation and reach senior levels. The industry has been labeled as one of misconduct or theft.

All bartenders developed a mindset that they steal. Why? Recently, while working extensively in the wedding space and collaborating with some of the top industrialists and families, the first question invariably posed to me was, "Do your bartenders drink or steal liquor?" Sometimes, I have no answers because it is a harsh reality of our industry. I have caught staff under the influence or stealing items as small as soda cans in their bags on several occasions. When I ask them why, they have no answer. Despite earning a decent income as bartenders, a can's cost is insignificant for them, yet they have developed this habit. I remain on a quest to understand the psychology behind these actions.

There have been stances, under which I want to confront my customers by pointing out that in a wedding of 1,000 people, where 300 people are from outside vendors, they still want to check the bags or question the bartenders or chefs about stealing, as if all the other 250 people have washed their sins! However, it is nobody's fault, yet at the same time, everybody's fault. We have created these mindsets in the consumer's mind.

India is the largest consumer and producer of liquor in the world and has an even bigger market for counterfeit liquor within the country. Rumour has it, that the total Black Label whisky produced globally is less than the amount consumed in India alone. However, we cannot start a blame game over who initiated this. It appears we have created a demand for counterfeit products to infiltrate the system, like the great Albert Einstein said, "Whatever the mind can conceive, it can achieve."

Given the cut-throat competition and the losing proposition in the bar business, there is a rampant need to create shortcuts to achieve profitability, and the liquor system has developed those solutions. Most bartenders are offered attractive prices for empty bottle cases and caps from the closing bars to earn extra income. The staff likely thinks, "I'll be able to cover my transportation costs if I take some caps." The problem does not lie with the individuals creating those re-bottling units; it is the system that demands and provides them with the raw materials to produce counterfeit liquor. They cannot operate alone.

I believe education is paramount for any industry to evolve. The entire chain of command needs to rediscover and rethink how to approach the model so that all stakeholders benefit, and we create a sustainable and profitable business model to attract global investors, not just unorganized or marginal ones.

❢ SUGGESTIONS ❢

✓ A thorough audit conducted by an independent body is imperative to assess procedures, safety standards, and the sourcing of liquor, thereby distinguishing between establishments adhering to high standards and those that fall short.

✓ The active involvement of owners in collaboration with the management team is crucial for gaining insight into operational challenges and facilitating timely reinvestment in processes and infrastructure.

✓ Incidents of misconduct and theft must be met with stern repercussions to deter future occurrences. Establishing clear accountability and responsibility is essential in maintaining integrity.

✓ Prioritizing the training and development of both the management team and staff should be a foundational objective, with allocated funds dedicated to this purpose within the Food & Beverage sector. Empowering managers to make urgent financial decisions is paramount.

✓ Educating customers about the presence of counterfeit liquor is vital, encouraging them to insist on authentic products from F&B outlets. Instances of counterfeit liquor should be promptly reported to the relevant authorities.

2

The Troubled State of Restaurant and Bar Work Culture

"Speaking of competition in the fast-food industry.
This is rat eat rat, dog eat dog. I'll kill 'em, and I'm
going to kill 'em before they kill me".
– Ray Kroc, Ex-CEO, Mcdonald's

The hospitality owners have been labeled as pursuing a rich man's hobby, with rampant use of unaccounted money and bribed in the construction of most civil projects. Opening restaurants and bars has become a money laundering business, where black money is used to build lavish establishments. With the proposed GST at 5 percent and no input tax credit, owners are increasingly using cash for purchasing raw materials and paying salaries, while most of the revenue is converted into white money by paying the 5 percent GST. So, who benefits ultimately, and who doesn't?

My interaction with most employees or staff have been that they have never received an offer letter or proper employment certificate due to ambiguity over salary payments, let alone any PF or medical insurance for their staff. When asked about training and development after working over 12-hour shifts, nobody had a clue.

The staff are made to work long hours without following any minimum wage act or employee benefits. When a mistake is made, or if the owner has mismanaged operations, the ultimate sufferers remain the employees with unpaid salaries. I have witnessed numerous instances where staff have not been paid salaries for months or even collected service charges for months. In one instance, a senior staff member, was told to leave without being paid for three months of salary. After following up with the owner directly for six months, he received no reply. It reminded me of the airline industry, in which a brand known as Kingfisher Airlines, went bankrupt where staff went unpaid for over six months. In that case, however, the airline had huge bank loans, and there was no cash in the business to pay liabilities, as per the figures.

While most owners have a strong real estate and construction business running in the background, which itself has remained unorganized, they have extended the same practices to the hospitality industry. Having worked in the investment banking industry for over six months before finding my passion in this field, I remain in awe of how the industry has been operating. After working 4 to 5 companies in my professional career in the financial market, I still have a folder with all the documents from each employer and salary slips. However, I have yet to interview a person for be profile of hospitality staff member who has complete documentation or even a proper salary slip.

When I say "most," I mean there are a few conglomerates or brands funded by institutions or investors who have adhered to professional standards and employee benefits. However, when I speak of the unorganized players with 1 to 15-20 outlets, a significant divide is underway. We see a large pool of employees stuck below the minimum salary bracket. They have nothing to spare beyond basic necessities. This might be a reason behind the misconduct and theft within the industry, as frustration has reached a boiling point after a certain period.

❕ SUGGESTIONS ❕

✓ An authoritative governing body should be established to enforce stringent labor laws and mandatory medical benefits for employees, along with robust employment agreements aimed at minimizing attrition and ensuring long-term staff stability.

✓ Employers should prioritize the implementation of comprehensive HR policies, including thorough documentation and reference checks for prospective employees. Mandatory police verification should be conducted as part of the hiring process.

✓ Employees should provide a proper handover to their previous employer before receiving a full and final settlement letter. Furthermore, employers should maintain a clear record of employment history to prevent unauthorized employment elsewhere.

✓ It is imperative that all financial records of F&B brands or cafes are meticulously maintained to demonstrate clean accounting practices for future fundraising and bank financing. Proper documentation of assets and vendor contracts is essential to mitigate disputes, a common reason for the closure of many establishments.

✓ Prior to entering into a partnership, partners should establish a clear understanding and define responsibilities to prevent conflicts and disputes in the future.

3

Reality vs. Expectations: The Trap

"Today I see a billion people as a billion potential consumers, an opportunity to generate value for them and to make a return for myself".
"It is important to achieve our goals, but not at any cost."
– Mukesh Ambani, CEO & Chairman of Reliance Industries

The F&B industry is valued at a whopping USD 247 billion and is expected to grow by 13-14 percent annually for the next five years. The F&B industry can be classified into several sub-segments, including dairy, confectionary, frozen foods, alcoholic and non-alcoholic beverages, etc. The food service industry, slated at USD 57.2 billion according to Wazir Advisors, accounts for only USD 5.9 billion from organized chains, which is a mere 10 percent of the total food service market.

India is expected to move among the top five business travel markets globally by 2030. However, the F&B sector is stuck in a plethora of challenges, including the turnaround time, as more than 10 licenses are required to open and run a restaurant business, ranking below countries like China, Turkey, Thailand, and Singapore. There are significant issues with rising infrastructure costs, instability over government regulations, and nearly zero funding through banking channels.

A friend from the USA, who owns one of the premium F&B brands in Delhi, has an outlet in one of the posh areas of the city, has opened over three Indian restaurants in the San Francisco Bay Area and is doing extremely well, but refuses to expand in India. When asked about why he is not expanding in India vis-à-vis the USA, the answer was an eye-opener.

He travels almost every two months for meetings, interviews, and paperwork formalities for hiring Indian chefs. He realized that opening an Indian restaurant outside of India is a clear winner due to the huge labor arbitrage between developed countries. As a norm in the USA, the landlord shares a certain percentage of the capital expenditure for a restaurant, and after establishing a certain brand image in the market, you can access bank financing very easily at 4-5 percent against your revenue and assets, ensuring your brand never suffers in mobilisation of funds.

In India, getting a loan against a restaurant is quite hard, leading to a heavy dependency on individual investors or unorganized players. Given the challenge of running a restaurant succesfully for more than 4-5 years, investors are usually looking to invest their surplus unaccounted money in the business, in addition to the glamour associated with owning an F&B brand.

Apart from this, due to the under-penetration of technology in the F&B sector, many restaurants and bars suffer from a lack of management skills and pilferage issues. Since most staff members do not have a relevant background or education in hotel management, they often resort to shortcuts to achieve the desired results. Most hiring is done by managers appointing their acquaintances and previous co-workers to avoid exposing weaknesses to the owners.

Owners continuously doubt their staff regarding pilferage, leading to mistrust in management. The staff hides deficiencies and presents a rosy picture of operations, when the owners visits. I have seen a few brands driven by technology and processes, like the Yum Yum Tree Group and Olive Group, which are extremely professional with their management and strict about delivering customer experiences, making them very profitable.

Apart from restaurants, most new-age bars and clubs heavily depend on the younger generation for their sales, as there are limited avenues for underage patrons to enjoy out-of-home experiences. With the advent of smoking zones, families are continuously avoiding these spaces due to the lack of a decent atmosphere. I believe, as in other countries, there should be separate smoking and non-smoking zones, allowing brands to expand their offerings and customer base and reducing their dependence on a particular customer segment.

On one occasion, on the way to visiting a city mall, I noticed a dhaba packed with a waiting crowd, whereas most new-age cafes with lavish ambiances and loud lighting were hardly crowded despite numerous influencers posing on every photobooth area. In today's world, the value of quality food and value for money is losing importance. Recently, I saw a viral reel on Instagram where a guy joked that if you want your enemy to go bankrupt, pray for them to open a bar or restaurant.(blanket statements)

❡ SUGGESTIONS ❡

These are pragmatic strategies for enhancing the efficiency and success of F&B concepts:

- ✓ **Focus on Concept Development:** Prioritize the development of innovative F&B concepts over extravagant interiors. Invest in unique culinary experiences that resonate with customers rather than solely focusing on lavish ambiance.

- ✓ **Financial Prudence:** Practice meticulous financial planning and maintain expenditure within reasonable limits. Prioritize logical spending over unnecessary extravagance to ensure sustainable business operations.

- ✓ **Diverse Customer Zones:** Designate separate areas to cater to diverse customer demographics, including families and older individuals with greater disposable income. Tailor concepts to appeal to a broad market reach for sustained profitability.

- ✓ **Authentic Feedback Channels:** Emphasize genuine customer feedback over influencer endorsements. Implement robust feedback management systems to gather insights and improve service quality based on real customer experiences.

- ✓ **Investment in Technology:** Allocate resources to invest in technology for business operations. Leverage automation and streamlined processes to introduce new products and enhance efficiency, reducing reliance on manual management.

- ✓ **Merit-Based Staffing:** Select staff based on their skills and performance rather than solely relying on references. Foster a culture of meritocracy to ensure the recruitment of competent and motivated employees.

✓ **Senior Management Involvement:** Encourage senior management participation and accountability by offering profit-sharing or ESOPs. Maintain transparency in financial matters to foster trust and encourage broader employee engagement in the company's success.

By implementing these strategies, F&B concepts can optimize operations, enhance customer satisfaction, and achieve sustainable growth in a competitive market environment.

❑❑❑

4

Leveraging Gaps &
Opportunities for Profitability

*"Human capital is the most precious of all forms
of capital available".*
– Ajay Ramasubramaniam, Ryerson Futures Inc.

As our nation opens its doors to the world, the hospitality sector finds itself at a crossroad, grappling with a lack of exposure to international tourism. Unlike their counterparts in Western nations, where the hospitality industry enjoys robust engagement with global visitors. Indian hospitality workers face stark disparities in salaries, compensation and working conditions. In developed countries, staff is rewarded handsomely, often earning five to ten times the salaries of their Indian counterparts, alongside a robust tipping culture and more manageable work shifts.

Over the next decade, under the visionary leadership of the incumbent Prime Minister, *Sh. Narendra Modi* there lies a huge potential for a seismic shift in India's tourism landscape, one that could manifest our hospitality industry to a global audience. Failure to adequately address this transition could lead to harsh criticism and negative publicity. Despite a willingness to invest extravagantly in restaurant and bar aesthetics, there exists a troubling hesitancy when it comes to allocating resources for essential equipment or staff welfare.

Our education system urgently requires reform, while owners must recalibrate their mindset to recognize and invest in the talent of their workforce. Salaries within the hospitality sector are increasingly disparate, particularly on the beverage side, exacerbating an already challenging crisis. The absence of reputable institutions catering to hospitality education further compounds the issue, leaving HR managers and owners ill-equipped to discern between potential and mediocrity.

Faced with the glaring wage disparity between India and developed nations, the allure of international business opportunities becomes irresistible, tempting many skilled individuals to seek greener pastures abroad. The exodus of top talent to destinations like Dubai, Singapore, Hong Kong, and the United States leaves our domestic industry scrambling to fill critical roles.

Current conditions are unsustainable, with many establishments operating on thin margins or merely breaking even. Despite heavy investments in aesthetics and marketing, it is the staff that bears the brunt of the industry's challenges, enduring long shifts and navigating unreasonable expectations from both patrons and proprietors.

While a few establishments prioritize delivering memorable experiences over discount-driven strategies, the industry at large faces significant hurdles that are often ignored or dismissed. Whether driven by insecurity, resignation, or personal animosity, industry insiders often turn a blind eye to these pressing issues, perpetuating a cycle of exploitation and discontent among staff.

In conclusion, addressing the gaping disparities and systemic challenges within the hospitality industry is imperative for its long-term viability and prosperity. This demands a fundamental shift in mindset among owners, a commitment to investing in staff welfare and professional development, and a steadfast dedication to delivering unparalleled guest experiences.

Reflecting on the stark contrasts in wages between Europe and India, where the average hourly rate stands at a substantial EUR 24, yielding approximately INR 3 lakh per month, a commendable figure conducive to a healthy work-life balance, one can't help but acknowledge the glaring disparities. Understandably, higher taxes and elevated living standards in developed nations contribute to this chasm. Conversely, the starting salary for a bartender in India, particularly in South India, presents a grim reality. In places like Kochi, where the initial pay dwindles to a mere INR 13,000, bartenders find themselves trapped with limited options.

Conversations with proprietors of bar institutes reveal a disheartening truth: despite the presence of immensely talented individuals, the reluctance to pursue careers in bartending persists. The dwindling enrollment numbers—barely reaching 4 to 5 students—paint a somber picture, contrasting sharply with the desperate calls from bar owners in search of skilled bartenders.

The exodus of top talent abroad, coupled with a dearth of incentives to retain or attract skilled professionals, underscores the industry's struggle to reach its full potential. The stagnant growth, fueled by a clientele primarily comprising Indians weary of repetitive experiences or the absence of innovative offerings, perpetuates a cycle of mediocrity. Sadly, the majority of restaurants and bars across the country languish in unprofitability, their returns scarcely surpassing those of a conservative bank deposit.

Drawing from firsthand experiences in the bar industry, an alarming revelation unfolds: the intricate arithmetic of profitability fails to add up. Discount-driven competition, epitomized by platforms like Zomato, exerts immense pressure on revenue streams, disregarding the essence of the dining experience. Emphasis on celebrity appearances and lavish presentations further diverts resources, leaving little room for staff welfare. Consequently, it is the staff that bear the brunt of clientele tantrums and laborious shifts, resorting to shortcuts amid the chaos, only to be scapegoat by owners.

In acknowledging these challenges, it becomes evident that such grievances cannot be dismissed as isolated incidents. However, amidst the prevailing disillusionment, glimmers of hope emerge in the form of brands that prioritize experiential excellence over discounts. Yet, discussions with industry insiders yield little resolution, often shrouded in apathy, insecurity, or outright hostility.

In closing, the road ahead is fraught with challenges, yet brimming with potential for transformation. To navigate this terrain successfully, a collective commitment to confronting these disparities head-on is imperative. Only then can the industry realize its true promise and flourish, offering both patrons and professionals alike an experience worth savoring.

SUGGESTIONS

These are excellent initiatives aimed at enhancing talent management and development within the F&B industry:

✓ **Improved Employee Packages:** Offer attractive packages to top talents, including competitive salaries and long-term growth plans. Provide opportunities for career advancement and professional development to retain skilled employees.

✓ **Reverse Brain Drain Strategy:** Implement a strategy to attract top talent from around the world, offering senior management roles with clear accountability and responsibility. Link salary packages to business growth to incentivize performance.

✓ **Enhanced Training Programs:** Collaborate with industry stakeholders and training institutes to enhance training and development programs for F&B establishments. Foster collective initiatives to improve skill development and knowledge sharing.

✓ **Centralized Employment Database:** Establish a centralized database of training institutes to connect F&B brands with potential employment opportunities. Streamline the recruitment process and facilitate career growth for aspiring professionals.

✓ **Empowerment for Staff:** Encourage creativity and decision-making among staff members to invest in business growth and uphold hospitality standards. Provide autonomy to employees to contribute ideas and initiatives for continuous improvement.

✓ **Utilization of Technology:** Leverage technology to optimize workforce efficiency and drive profitability. Focus on upskilling employees and implementing multitasking capabilities to achieve leaner operations while maintaining service quality.

By implementing these initiatives, the F&B industry can foster a culture of talent development, innovation, and efficiency, ultimately leading to sustainable growth and success.

5

Keeping the Food on the Table

"The fast-food industry is notorious for employing millions of Americans at poverty wages".
– David Rolf, American Strategist

In the pursuit of novel dining experiences, I find myself grappling with a disconcerting truth: while culinary concepts evolve and cuisines fuse, the essence of food—its quality and preparation—often remains neglected. Restaurateurs, fixated on creating visually stunning, Instagram-worthy dishes, resort to excessive use of butter and frying to tantalize taste buds. It's a familiar sight: ubiquitous offerings like chicken tikka or butter chicken grace menus across establishments, distinguished solely by ambiance, presentation, and background music. In this landscape, brand perception hinges more on superficial elements than on the actual culinary experience. With resources poured into grandiose décor and elaborate settings, the heart and soul of F&B take a backseat.

Contemplating the trajectory of the industry, I'm left pondering its direction. While abroad, I eagerly explore local cuisines, shying away from Indian fare. Yet, I can't help but notice that Indian restaurants abroad, when offering authentic experiences, are teeming with expats, drawn to the allure of

Indian flavors. The irony isn't lost on me: expatriates flock to savor our cuisine, making dishes like chicken tikka masala the pride of nations like Britain. However, I can't shake the apprehension that these same expats, upon returning to our shores, may find themselves disillusioned by an industry more focused on aesthetics than authenticity.

In an era dominated by Quick Service Restaurants (QSRs), even traditional eateries adopt a similar modus operandi. Dark kitchens proliferate, churning out ready-to-eat meals at an unprecedented pace. These establishments prioritize efficiency over craftsmanship, with dishes precooked and simply reheated upon order, all at a price point designed to lure in customers. This results in a diminished reliance on skilled chefs and a compromise on culinary excellence to meet the demands of a fast-paced market.

The harrowing reality of our industry's working conditions fuels a vicious cycle of turnover. Staff turnover rates soar as employees seek greener pastures, enticed by the promise of higher wages or a more prestigious brand next door. New owners, eager to emulate the success of their neighbors, poach talent with the hope of bolstering sales. Yet, as reality sets in, disillusionment ensues, and once-promising careers veer off course amid clashes of ego and misaligned expectations.

In the end, it's the staff that bear the brunt of industry turbulence, their livelihoods hanging in the balance amidst the whims of owners. As we navigate this tumultuous landscape, it becomes imperative to recalibrate our priorities, such as authenticity and fostering a nurturing environment for culinary talent to thrive. Only then can we truly elevate the dining experience and ensure a sustainable future for the F&B industry.

❙ SUGGESTIONS ❙

- ✓ **Focus on Mindfulness Cooking:** Use more methods involving live cooking and freshness, with a balanced diet approach.
- ✓ Discard ready-to-eat meals and frozen foods in the kitchen.
- ✓ Get to know the roots of Indian cuisine and include that in our menu concept.
- ✓ Focus on consistency of experience and quality of food rather than Instagram gimmicks.

6

New Age QSRs
Trapped in Fancy Gimmicks

*"We are spending millions, if not billions of dollars
every year on programs to fight the childhood obesity
epidemic while giving almost $2 billion of taxpayer
money to the junk food and fast food industries to
make the epidemic worse".*
– Dennis Kucinich, Former US Representative

In India, over seven million people work in the food and beverage (F&B) industry, making it the largest employer. However, while it's a significant part of the job market, it only contributes a small amount to the country's overall economy. Nevertheless, most shopping centers heavily rely on having good places to eat and drink. Nowadays, when new shopping centers are built, they ensure they include good movie theaters and F&B spots because they are seen as key to the mall's success.

New malls often offer F&B establishments favorable deals to set up shop there. They might provide financial assistance to help them start, and they might even waive rent at first. This helps F&B spots get started in the mall and attract customers. Big names like Haldiram sometimes secure very favorable deals to occupy the best spots. Many of the newer F&B places are focusing on big cities and areas near highways to secure good deals and reach a larger audience.

However, there's a problem once these new F&B spots open in malls. They spend a lot of money to set up, and then they're locked into long contracts with the mall. They might not be able to leave for years, even if they're struggling. And after a couple of years, when they have to start paying rent, it can become challenging for smaller establishments. Larger companies have more bargaining power to negotiate and secure better deals. The mall operators sign these leases on lucrative terms. This initially help them sell the shops to investors by showing the return on their investment of rental yield which will be paid by you after 2nd or 3rd years of operations at market rate. Sometimes the mall operators don't even bother about the construction since their primary purpose of signing the documents was to move their mall inventory to investors so the funds collected can be used to operationalize the mall.

F&B establishments have become a significant feature in shopping centers, with fancy decorations and marketing. Malls are promoting these spots alongside their other stores. They charge much higher rents for F&B spots as compared other spaces in the mall. Even movie theaters are accomodating to make more space for renting out to food places, which helps theaters to generate more revenue.

If you look at the financial performance of movie theaters, you'll notice that an increasing portion of their revenue comes from food and drinks, apart from tickets. They make a substantial profit from items like popcorn and soda, as they charge premium prices for them. This helps them increase their profit margins, along with the revenue they generate from renting out space to F&B establishments.

The new QSR formats offers a wide variety of cuisines and options without much focus on their core products. Most of the successful QSR formats, such as Dominos, McDonalds, KFC, Taco Bell, and many other international brands, have achieved global scale due to their relentless focus on a selective products and improving their quality and value-for-money proposition for customers.

I find it very interesting that every successful brand with quick order turnaround has a high probability of becoming successful. Even iconic regional brands in India, like *Tunday Kabab* from Lucknow or *Gol Gappa* from Bengali Market, are defined by one product that contributes to the majority of their profits and revenues, while the rest of the menu items may not even contribute to the bottom line and can create a diversion of limited resources.

For example, look at the case of Wow Momos, which pioneered the concept of selling street food Momos in a more hygienic format. They initially focused on one simple product, the momo, and diversified their menu with 50 different products to create variety. This strategy helped them achieve economies of scale in large-scale production of momos, leading to profitability in their initial stores. Wow Momos has now grown to over 600 outlets with multiple brands under the same umbrella.

Many brands including those which are based on North Indian cuisines are selling Chinese items, Adding Chinese items requires additional kitchen setup, a Chinese chef, specific cutlery, and maintaining inventory of raw materials, all of which can impact the profitability of the establishment. Meanwhile, leading establishments are including basic beverages like Coke, water, and Red Bull in their menus, even as their food menu extends to 200 items.

We need to evolve our thinking to recognize that food and beverages are two sides of the same coin and require equal attention in menu offerings. Abroad, I have observed fine dining restaurants focusing equally on beverages than their food menus, recognizing that beverages tend to be more profitable for F&B establishments.

❗ SUGGESTIONS ❗

✓ **Focus on your USP:** Prioritize quality over quantity.

✓ Minimize costs to the industry's minimum to ensure affordability for customers. Focus on the value-for-money concept to rapidly scale your business.

✓ Develop your concept extensively and build your menu around it. Avoid unrelated items on the menu.

✓ Implement processes and technology to automate delivery and ensure consistent product quality.

✓ Avoid falling into the real estate trap of accepting rent-free and upfront capex support from mall operators. Wait for the mall to achieve the necessary footfall to ensure viability for your operations.

✓ Engage a beverage consultant to build a robust beverage offering that complements your food menu to maximize revenue potential.

❑❑❑

7

Gaps in Bar Training and Hotel Management Colleges

"When I see someone either break free from the grips of the food industry, leave their job for something more meaningful, or start to be in a relationship that really helps them become who they're supposed to be, that inspires me".
–Vani Hari, American Author

More than half (∼ 68 percent) of hotel management graduates requires training from scratch since most hotel management institutes are not in synchronization with the current trends, challenges and demands of the F&B sector. There is a lack of implementation of a standard protocol or a unified authority to guide all hotel management colleges in upgrading their curriculum to industry standards. When it comes to beverages, there are only a handful of bar training institutes operating at the city level, unable to expand their operations beyond.

With most aspiring bartenders viewing this career path as a way out of poverty, they have very little scope to pay hefty fees, leading to less investment by institute owners in infrastructure capabilities for their students. There is a huge gap in F&B training, where International HM colleges have vast infrastructure. During my recent visit to the *Pradhan Mantri Kaushal Vikas Kendra*, which operates under the aegis of the National Skill Development Corporation, they had beautiful classrooms, training facilities, and computer labs but had delisted bartending as a course due to the unavailability of faculty.

Private bar training institutes have some of the best bartending faculty and training modules, but the dependency on students to bear high fees and the lack of knowledge about bartending as a career lead to an unviable option. Most successful bartending institutes depends upon using their students for events to recover fees or having the students' fees sponsored by leading alcohol companies.

Private training institutes are struggling to effectively market themselves to prospective students and establish credibility for their certificates. Many of these institutes lack affiliations or associations that could enhance their credibility among potential employers.

Hotels, which are major employers of hospitality students, often rely on private hospitality colleges to supply them with students for their expansion plans. These jobs typically require minimal skill sets since much of the training happens on the job.

There is a significant lack of technology in our education system that could connect students with the right institutions. Social media, however, has the potential to reach even the most remote locations of our country and attract prospective students, including those from economically disadvantaged backgrounds, to enroll in private bartending or culinary institutes. These institutes often offer short-term courses at affordable price.

Hospitality jobs offer some of the best returns on student

investment in education. For example, an average bartending course lasting 3 months costs between INR 40,000 to INR 60,000. This investment enables prospective students to secure jobs paying between INR 18,000 to INR 25,000 in metro cities and INR 14,000 to INR 18,000 in smaller towns shortly after completing the course. The payback period is 3-6 months, the shortest across all industries.

In terms of associations, we recognize the NRAI (National Restaurant Association of India) as the body for restaurant owners in India. However, there is still no institution or association governing employees in the hospitality industry in India. Furthermore, none of the Indian bodies are associated with international organizations to provide recognition for the Indian hospitality sector.

For instance, the International Bartenders Association (IBA), founded in 1951 in the United Kingdom, includes over 67 member countries or associations worldwide, including smaller nations like Armenia, Ecuador, Estonia, Latvia, Serbia, Vietnam, and many others. India has yet to become a member. India has never represented itself in their Annual General Meeting held annually, attended by all member countries except in 2019 in Tokyo when India was represented by Late. *Pankaj Kamble* through India Bartenders Guild.

India's participation in IBA competitions twice in Taiwan and Singapore through the India Bartender's Guild (IBG) resulted in Indian representatives achieving significant achievement despite starting from a lower position in the competition. This is a big alarm for our crumbling industry and there is an immediate need for leadership to guide the industry in the right direction.

Bartending competitions held in India are largely dominated by alcohol companies that heavily fund these events to influence bartenders to endorse their brands in F&B establishments. These competitions typically take place in 5-star hotels accompanied by impressive PR activities. Participants are often invited or selected from leading cocktail bars in metro cities.

Unfortunately, most competitions exclude newcomers and students. There is a recurring trend where winners are often affiliated with leading alcohol brands as their top customers, well-connected to their teams, or have received significant grooming in the past.

There is currently no platform for mid-level bartenders or students to showcase their talent in competitions. Many talented individuals face career stagnation due to inadequate opportunities and lack of support from their immediate circles.

Similar trends are observed in flair bartending competitions, where events often feature established or renowned flair bartenders, with few opportunities given to new talent to showcase their skills.

In our institute, we recently enrolled a student who is only 17 years old. While he qualifies for non-alcohol classes and flair training until he turns 18, within just one month of practice, he has proven to be one of the best flair bartenders in our institute. In fact, he demonstrates skills surpassing those of our experienced flair trainers. With proper guidance, I am confident he could compete at the highest levels of flair bartending by the age of 20.

On the other hand, another flair bartender with exceptional talents, trained extensively, having attempted various ventures including bartending institutes and running his own bar catering company, faced continuous setbacks. Eventually, he shifted his career path to organic farming.

Jobs in hospitality, especially in private restaurants and bars, often include large variable components in the form of service charges distributed to employees based on their rank. This variable component can be as high as 20-25% of the fixed component, further enhancing the job profile. Professions like bartenders and butlers can also collect substantial tips for providing excellent service on busy nights.

The beverage industry within QSR brands is experiencing a significant talent shortage amidst aggressive expansion efforts. Many brands struggle to develop or source talent specifically for their beverage offerings. As a result, there is a growing demand for Ready to Drink (RTD) products in cans or bottles at these QSR brands. They are increasingly focusing on food while expanding their beverage offerings through RTD options prominently displayed.

Most RTD products are priced in two tiers – one for retail and another for QSRs/Hotels, which is typically nearly double the normal MRP. This higher pricing allows hotels and QSRs to maintain larger margins to offset their higher fixed costs.

⸙ SUGGESTIONS ⸙

✓ There is a need to create a unified bartending association to bring all private bartending institutes under one umbrella, providing them with recognition and enhancing the credibility of their courses.

✓ IHM colleges should collaborate with private bartending and chef institutes to facilitate industry-leading knowledge sharing and update their curriculum to meet industry standards.

✓ Private institutes should heavily invest in digital marketing, such as SEO, Instagram, and Facebook ads, to reach states like Uttarakhand and the Northeast, which are significant resources for the hospitality industry.

✓ Private institutes should offer residential programs so that students from smaller towns can relocate and stay on campus, alleviating their parents' concerns.

✓ More job portals need to be established where small F&B establishments can connect with IHM colleges and private institutes to find prospective students.

✓ More Competition needs to be organized to promote students and new comers to participate and highlight talents. Inter IHM colleges competition should be organized to enable sharing of knowledge and giving exposure to students.

✓ Proper Professional bartender certification or introduction of bar license to existing bartenders pool to promote standardization of quality of manpower in our industry.

8

Growth *vs.* Reality in Weddings and Social Events

"1/5th of an individual life saving is spent on a wedding. In fact, 20% of all loan taken in India are for wedding only. Indians spend the entire 12 years of their hard-earned money in 2-3 days!"
– Nikhil Kamath, Founder Zerodha

The F&B sector in the event space is growing rapidly, especially with the wedding market expanding by 30 percent each year. In India, the wedding industry has become a massive USD 50 billion market, ranking second only to the USA internationally and the 4th largest industry in the country. Over the next 15 years, more than 40 crore weddings are expected, surpassing the total population of the US, which is around 32 crores. The trend of destination weddings is also on the rise, with nearly 1 in every 5 couples opting for this, thereby shifting a significant portion of the wedding market to premium hotels.

Many hotels in Jaipur, Udaipur, Jaisalmer, and Goa now rely on weddings or social events as major profit drivers. For instance, the Fairmont in Jaipur hosts over +100 weddings annually, often having back-to-back weddings on the same day during peak seasons. Consequently, the hotel lobby can resemble a bustling international airport during such times, with constant movement of bags, people, and staff working tirelessly. Despite the influx of weddings, the off-season workload for hotel staff seems never-ending.

A decade ago, alcohol was a rarity at weddings, with only basic brands available at makeshift counters. However, the industry has evolved significantly since then, with alcohol now being a central focus of many weddings. Premium brands, elaborated bar setups, inspired by platforms like Pinterest, have become common features at lavish weddings. However, there is often a discrepancy between the promised bar designs and the actual setups at events.

The shortage of skilled manpower in the F&B space for events has led business owners to emphasize on decor, presentation, and, uniforms to assure quality to wedding families. Similarly, on the beverage side, fancy props and structures are used to conceal the lack of expertise among beverage professionals. The event industry is characterized by extreme stress and long hours, with staff often unaware of their roles until they reach the event site.

From a sustainability perspective, the event business faces significant challenges, particularly in terms of food wastage. Lavish wedding menus often include excessive items, leading to a substantial amount of leftover food being wasted. This wastage contrasts starkly with the sight of underprivileged children sleeping hungry on the streets.

Addressing these disparities and implementing fair business practices is essential for the long-term growth and sustainability of the F&B industry in hospitality. By fostering positive vibes and ensuring sound business operations, the industry can overcome it's struggles and achieve greater success.

❘ SUGGESTIONS ❘

✓ Leftover food should be properly disposed of through NGOs to support street families.

✓ Reduce the wedding menu to a limited selection and accurately forecast consumption to minimize wastage at each event.

✓ Transform seasonal business operations into year-round operations to enable F&B establishments to invest in full-time staff rather than relying solely on freelance staff during peak periods.

✓ Emphasize the bar concept and the quality of drinks over the décor of the bar.

✓ Ensure vendors provide comprehensive contracts to clients to establish clear expectations and discourage last-minute requests from wedding parties, reducing stress and ensuring adherence to pre-determined commitments.

✓ Hotels should hire additional staff during peak wedding seasons to alleviate pressure on existing full-time hotel staff.

✓ Conduct thorough background checks on vendors by wedding planners, including assessments of their offices/warehouses, track records, licenses, and whether they employ full-time staff or rely on freelancers, to prevent subpar service delivery during peak periods.

9

The Role of Influencers in F&B

"Take criticism seriously, but not personally. If there is truth or merit in the criticism, try to learn from it. Otherwise, let it roll right off you".
– Hillary Clinton, Former US SoS

Recently, the impact of influencers has become pronounced in the F&B industry. Many owners now focus on making their brands go viral on platforms like Instagram, catering to the demands of fashion and food bloggers with large follower counts, even though they are aware that influencers alone may not significantly increase footfall.

In my own experience with a QSR brand, I've encountered instances where social media influencers insisted for free meals and even requested complimentary Uber rides afterward. Intrigued by this, I explored fake follower agencies and was surprised to find that large follower counts could be purchased at very low prices.

On another occasion, while organizing a Pub Crawl, I was advised to invite specific influencers with high follower counts. However, it later became apparent that some of these influencers were friends who had manipulated the situation to attend the event for free under the guise of networking.

Despite such encounters, there are genuine influencers who create authentic content and garner real followings. It's essential to discern between fake and genuine influencers by examining their content.

For new owners, it's advisable to invite influencers with genuine networks who provide honest reviews of your establishment. I often receive requests from underage individuals seeking barter collaborations, which I choose to ignore.

In the event and festival space, influencers often play significant roles in gaining free entry alongwith food and beverages. During my last Cocktail Week, I observed that the guest list comprised a significant number of influencers and industry experts, surpassing ticketed sales. Many F&B ventures are struggling due to a lack of content and experience, despite appearances suggesting otherwise.

Besides, food bloggers are shifting towards fashion and travel blogging due to higher budgets offered by apparel brands. As influencers increasingly turn to other industries for growth, larger consumer brands are allocating dedicated marketing budgets towards influencers, leading to improved financial well-being for genuine content creators.

❚ SUGGESTIONS ❚

Here are some suggestions to enhance your social media engagement and ensure authenticity in collaborations:

✓ **Engage Content Creators:** Instead of solely relying on food bloggers or influencers, consider collaborating with content creators who specialize in creating engaging and authentic content across various platforms.

✓ **Trendy Reels with Social Media Team:** Utilize your social media team to create trending reels featuring your team and behind-the-scenes moments. This can help your content go viral and increase engagement.

✓ **Authenticity Check:** Invest in software tools that can assess the authenticity of followers and provide insights into the breakdown of fake versus real followers. This ensures that your collaborations are with genuine influencers who can reach your target audience effectively.

✓ **Insight Details from Collaborators:** Require each collaborator to share their Instagram insights details, including reach and engagement metrics, for similar content they have posted. This helps validate their effectiveness in reaching your desired audience.

✓ **Feedback for Improvement:** Encourage unbiased opinions on your F&B offerings and use constructive feedback as a catalyst for improvement. Engage with customers and collaborators to understand their perspectives and areas for enhancement.

✓ **Differentiated Offering Guidance:** Guide content creators on your unique offerings in the market, emphasizing food quality over discount offers. Highlighting what sets your brand apart can attract genuine interest from followers.

✓ **PR Agency Engagement:** Consider hiring a PR agency to manage engagement with influencers and provide comprehensive reports on their authentic coverage and audience reach. This ensures transparency and accountability in your collaborations.

By implementing these suggestions, one can foster genuine engagement on social media, strengthen your brand presence, and build lasting relationships with both influencers and customers.

◻◻◻

10
RTD Beverages: The Next Growth Opportunity

"The fast-food industry has moved into the grocery store, so you no longer have to go to a fast-food chain to find problematic foods".
– Michael Moss, American Author

The beverage industry in the United States is valued at USD 146 billion, encompassing both non-alcoholic and alcoholic beverage production and distribution. One major trend is the focus on functional waters, as post-pandemic consumers have increasingly reduced sugar intake and opt for still or sparkling waters, or herb-infused varieties.

Another emerging trend is the innovation in alcoholic RTD (Ready-to-Drink) space and mocktails which expected to reach a value of USD 19.46 billion by 2027. The emphasis is on appealing flavors that are low in sugar and alcohol content.

There has been rapid progress in new product development, including hybrid combinations like sparkling waters infused with natural caffeine from tea and juice flavors. In India, for example, Raw Pressary has introduced Mint Mojito Iced Tea, combining elements of a Mojito mocktail with extracts from black and green tea for caffeine.

In the US market, coffee and tea consumption is on the rise due to reduced mobility and increased work-from-home arrangements, creating demand for convenient RTD brands. The market is projected to surpass USD 133 billion by 2027, with RTD beverages typically sold in cans, bottles, and tetrapacks for portability.

New consumers are gravitating towards dairy-free, plant-based alternatives and sugar-free options, prompting leading brands to introduce less or zero sugar variants. In India, the non-alcoholic beverage market is dominated by carbonated drinks and bottled water, expected to grow significantly by 2030.

Despite the potential, the industry faces challenges such as negative perceptions, high taxation under GST, logistical costs, environmental impacts, and counterfeit products from the unorganized sector. High taxes, particularly under GST, affect all carbonated drinks regardless of sugar levels, akin to alcohol and tobacco.

Several brands and startups, like Jade Forest, Sepoy, and Raw Pressary, are expanding rapidly and securing funding from domestic, angel, and international investors. However, profitability remains elusive for many brands trapped in a cycle of fundraising to meet growth targets.

Modern retail outlets often demand hefty upfront premiums and high margins, leaving little for marketing expenses. Established players like Coke and Pepsi dominate, making it challenging for new entrants due to higher GST on carbonated drinks and economies of scale.

Nonetheless, innovative brands like Paper Boat are introducing affordable beverage solutions and gaining market share. Labeling is becoming increasingly important, especially with health concerns over sugar content, prompting a shift towards zero sugar options.

In Southeast Asian countries like Thailand, the Philippines, and Singapore zero sugar and calorie options for iced tea, water-based drinks, and coffee variants are popular among daily commuters, with stevia and monk fruit emerging as healthy alternatives to sugar.

There's a significant growth opportunity for local brands if they can match global pricing, implement sustainable packaging, food standards and deploy innovative marketing strategies to compete with larger brands. We speak about guerilla marketing in the end which is rarely seen in the Indian market while most of the largest F&B brands globally have used guerilla marketing as an effective method to gain significant market share in a highly competitive world.

> *Red Bull is the world's most popular energy drink, dominating the global market share, selling millions of cans annually across nearly 100 countries. It has become a renowned case study in successful guerrilla marketing strategies worldwide. Red Bull's success can be attributed to its focus on advertising, extreme sports sponsorships, efficient distribution networks, innovative marketing campaigns, and continuous product innovation, all of which have significantly contributed to its status as one of the most beloved brands globally.*

❘ SUGGESTIONS ❘

- ✓ Move away from traditional marketing methods through HORECA and modern retail. Instead, focus on digital marketing and guerrilla marketing tactics.

- ✓ Highlight the USP of your product. Avoid attempting to replicate existing products and expecting similar success. Successful brands are built on effective marketing and brand positioning, rather than solely on product features.

- ✓ Emphasize healthy options for Ready-to-Drink (RTD) products and reduce dependence on sugary drinks.

- ✓ Prioritize unit economics and ensure the correct product-market fit before heavily investing in marketing or launching your product.

- ✓ Reduce reliance on external fundraising from angel investors and institutional funds during the early stages. Such funding often comes with aggressive marketing expectations and high burnout rates. Instead, focus on gradually building a profitable brand over time.

❑❑❑

11

How Technology is Taking Away Share from Traditional F&B Industry

"People will forget what you said. They will forget what you did. But they will never forget how you made them feel".
– Maya Angelou, American Activist

Zomato was conceptualized in 2008 as an online aggregator and has since become one of the most successful startups in the F&B space, boasting a market cap of USD 20 billion with just USD 800 million in annual revenue. Zomato's average monthly restaurants partner skyrocket from 61,000 in FY19 to 270,000 by FY24 along with over 5300 listed quick service restaurants (QSR). Through innovative marketing strategies and the convenience of ordering at the click of a button, Zomato has catalyzed the rise of dark kitchens, allowing new F&B ventures to forego expensive real estate and operate from remote locations. Coupled with deep discounting, this has enticed customers to shift from traditional dining experiences to ordering from a sleek app interface.

In a market dominated by Zomato and Swiggy, commission rates have surged from 8-10 percent to over 27 percent. However, the actual cost to restaurants extends beyond commissions, with hidden expenses and marketing tactics squeezing traditional F&B establishments to offer deep discounts while still paying hefty fees to online aggregators. Consequently, customers often enjoy lower prices at home compared to dining in-person at the same restaurants.

Restaurants may rationalize the arrangement by assuming that orders through Zomato and Swiggy represent incremental business from new customers. However, from a customer psychology perspective, many loyal patrons who once frequented these establishments now opt for the convenience of online ordering, saving up to 15-20 percent on their orders.

Consider a scenario, where a loyal customer orders a Mutton Kakori Roll from Khan Chacha, an iconic brand known for its rolls. It's unlikely that a customer would discover such an iconic brand on an online aggregator platform. Despite this, Zomato, leveraging its technological prowess, effectively extracts the majority of the profit margin from the iconic brand, leaving a mere 5 percent for every order fulfilled. The brand may mistakenly believe that they've only covered the food cost and gained a new customer, unaware of the significant loss in profit margin.

Khan Chacha	Menu Listing	Zomato Listing
Mutton Kakori Roll	309	309
GST (5%)	11.45	11.45
Restaurant Packing Charge		11.45
Delivery Partner Fee		84
Platform Fee		5
Total Amount	320.45	420.9

Discount (40 pc upto 80)		80
Total Payable by customer	**320.45**	**340.9**
Total Received by Brand	**320.45**	**146**
Recovery by brand	100%	43%
Recovery by Aggregator	0%	57%
Food Costing by brand	35%	38%
Profit Margin	65%	5%

When we delve into the implicit costs associated with fulfilling orders through online aggregators like Zomato, the scenario becomes complex. Consider a bustling Saturday night at Khan Chacha's outlet in Khan Market, known for its iconic rolls. Amidst the sophisticated clientele, a loyal customer eagerly awaits his Mutton Kakori Roll at the cash counter. Despite placing the order earlier and paying in full, the cashier or chef may prioritize fulfilling an online order that arrived later, prompted by Zomato's technology. Zomato monitors the average turnaround time for orders and alerts the manager about potential delays, which could impact their platform rating and future orders. Consequently, the dine-in customer, who has patiently waited, may find themselves sidelined in favor of online orders, thereby diminishing their dining experience and potentially leading them to reconsider their dining preferences.

Reflecting on my experience in Green Park Market, I recall the perplexing sight of an empty Domino's outlet amidst the bustling marketplace. Intrigued, I ventured inside to place a dine-in order for a Margarita pizza, only to be informed that they were exclusively catering to online orders due to overwhelming demand. The cashier revealed a stack of 25 kitchen order tickets (KOTs), highlighting the overwhelming shift towards online orders. Since then, I've exclusively ordered from Domino's through online platforms, unwittingly channeling the profit margins of a dine-in customer to Zomato's coffers, unbeknownst to the brand owner.

Over time, as restaurants witness a decline in walk-in customers, they may opt to relocate to cheaper premises or dark kitchens to cut costs and cater primarily to online orders. However, this exacerbates the trend of loyal customers transitioning to online platforms, further eroding the profitability of traditional dine-in establishments. The market capitalization of USD 20 billion achieved by Zomato comes at the expense of the 2 lakh restaurants and cafes that have seen a decline in their market value over time. This is a testament to the significant investment made by cafe owners in building their brand legacy over several decades.

During a recent family trip to Hyatt Dehradun, despite enjoying complimentary suite upgrades, our group found ourselves consistently ordering meals from unfamiliar brands through Zomato. Despite the convenience, we realized that our reliance on online ordering had shifted a significant portion of potential revenue from in-house dining to the aggregator. Despite the hotel's top-notch amenities and culinary expertise, its restaurants remained deserted, with Zomato riders frequenting the premises instead. The emergence of online aggregators like Zomato's Blinkit has further encroached on the market share of modern retail stores and hotel F&B outlets, presenting a formidable challenge to established players.

In conclusion, the F&B industry is grappling with the disruptive influence of online aggregators like Zomato, which has reshaped consumer behavior and eroded the profitability of traditional dine-in establishments. From empty restaurant premises to declining hotel F&B revenue, the impact of online aggregators is pervasive across the industry. As I explored opportunities to list FMCG products with modern retail outlets and online aggregators, I encountered significant barriers such as exorbitant upfront costs and commissions, highlighting the challenges faced by businesses navigating this evolving landscape. With a high failure rate among cafe and restaurants within the first year of operations, it's evident that inadequate capital and poor financial planning pose significant hurdles to industry newcomers.

❙ SUGGESTIONS ❙

✓ **Strategic Use of Online Aggregators:** Utilize online aggregator platforms strategically, maximizing revenue during non-peak hours while prioritizing loyal customers during peak hours. By focusing to serve loyal customers directly, brands can elevate their reputation through positive social media and word-of-mouth promotion.

✓ **Pricing Strategy:** Implement a pricing strategy that factors in the aggregator's commission. Consider reducing portion sizes or offering disclaimers to online customers, emphasizing that the experience may vary compared to dining in at the restaurant. This helps convey the value of the dine-in experience and encourages customers to visit the outlet.

✓ **Avoid Deep Discounting:** Resist the pressure to engage in deep discounting on online platforms, as this can compromise the quality and undermine the brand's reputation built over time. Instead, maintain pricing parity between online and walk-in customers, with online customers paying a premium for the convenience of home delivery.

✓ **Exclusive Dine-In Offerings:** Reserve Hero Products or specialty items exclusively for dine-in customers to preserve the authenticity and presentation of the dining experience. For example, high-end sushi dishes priced above a certain threshold may only be available for dine-in customers, enhancing the overall dining experience.

✓ **Regulation on Outside Food:** Implement restrictions on bringing outside food into hotels and 5-star properties to uphold hygiene standards and mitigate potential health risks. Establish designated areas within the hotel premises for consuming outside food, accompanied by clear disclaimers to minimize liabilities.

✓ **Policy for Hotel Bars and Restaurants:** Prohibit outside food and drinks in hotel bars and restaurants to maintain quality standards and uphold the exclusivity of the dining experience. Consider charging additional fees for serving and disposing of outside food to discourage customers from bringing their own food items.

✓ **Competitive Pricing and Creativity:** Embrace creativity and adjust pricing strategies to remain competitive with standalone restaurants. Focus on offering value-driven menus and promotions to attract volume and foster customer loyalty within the hotel's F&B outlets.

By implementing these strategies, F&B establishments can effectively leverage online aggregators while safeguarding their brand reputation and enhancing the overall dining experience for loyal customers.

❑❑❑

12

Obesity and Sugar Rush –An Epidemic

"People are fed by the food industry, which pays no attention to health, and are treated by the health industry, which pays no attention to food".
– Wendell Berry, American Novelist

According to the World Health Organization, obesity has tripled since 1975, with more than 1.9 billion overweight adults worldwide, of whom 650 million are obese. India is often referred to as the diabetic capital of the world. More people die from being overweight than from being underweight. The obesity epidemic has ensnared the younger generation, with over eight million children under the age of five being obese. One of the leading reasons for obesity and diabetes is the prevalence of lifestyle disorders related to inadequate sleep, unhealthy food and sugary drinks, excessive alcohol consumption, smoking, and drug abuse, coupled with negligible exercise. All of these factors are rampant among the youth and future generations, partly due to the influence of social media and peer pressure, enticing kids and youngsters into adopting unhealthy lifestyles to appear 'cool.'

In my own family, my mother was a diabetic patient who never took insulin, leading to a heart attack at the young age of

52. It has been almost 10 years since she passed, the tendency towards diabetes still persists in our bloodline. Recently, I have immersed myself in reading numerous self-help and health-related books, and have attended several wellness programs, which have enabled me to practice mindfulness and intermittent fasting regularly.

During a casual visit to modern retail outlets or food courts in malls, one is inundated with racks filled with sugar-laden drinks and ready-to-eat junk food. These sugar-laden drinks often mask their contents with various synonyms like fructose and sucrose, which are extremely detrimental to the body's immunity. In the Food and Beverage (F&B) industry, many beverage programs rely heavily on sugar-based syrups, often combined with soda and lime, unlike in Western countries where liquor-based flavors dominate cocktail menus. In India, sugar-based syrups are promoted heavily by brands and bar consultants to streamline recipes for high staff turnover, paralleling culinary practices that favor premade curry pastes and ready-to-use ingredients over fresh and plant-based options. To encourage repeat business, F&B outlets frequently use flour and excessive sugar to make their products addictive. Shockingly, India tops the charts for the highest sugar content in Coca-Cola cans compared to any other country globally. While developed nations prioritize regulating sugar levels in beverages, most South Asian countries offer zero-sugar options and promote healthier eating habits in their F&B brands.

There is an urgent need for Indian brands to champion healthy eating and drinking habits and to control portion sizes using fresh ingredients. Despite India's reputation as a culinary destination for global tourists, it has yet to earn Michelin star ratings for its restaurants, nor does it rank in the World's 50 Best Bars. Despite our rich cultural heritage deeply rooted in Ayurveda and spirituality, we often forsake our traditions in favor of Western influences in both diet and lifestyle.

Influencer Watch

Revant Himatsingkaaka Foodpharmer is becoming a YouTube sensation with below mentioned followers:

Youtube: 701k

Instagram: 1M

Twitter: 109k

He is on a mission to make 140 crore Indians health literate and does lot of humorous content talking about the healthy food and how package food lacks nutrition and aerated drinks are nothing but sugar drinks. He has done his MBA from Wharton, worked for Mckinsey in USA but left his job to pursue his mission. He travels with a lot of people while creating his content on social media.

Many celebrity chefs who have relocated abroad advocates for Jainism and satvic-inspired menus. Vikas Khanna, the celebrated Indian chef in New York, recently introduced a satvic food menu at the White House, promoting the Indian culinary experience in America. Several talented chefs have opened Indian restaurants abroad to cater to international tourists, while many Indian celebrity mixologists residing overseas have participated in festivals like Cocktail Week, eager to share their techniques with their homeland. However, it's worth noting that some specialty restaurants have faltered after promoting their head chefs to the status of owners, as the subsequent shift in focus often leads to a decline in restaurant growth.

! SUGGESTIONS !

These suggestions aim to foster healthier habits and environment within the Indian food and beverage industry:

- ✓ **Adopting a Slogan:** "Responsible Drinking, Responsible Eating" should become a guiding slogan for the Indian F&B industry, emphasizing the importance of mindful consumption.

- ✓ **Nutritional Disclosure:** The industry should embrace disclosing the nutritional value of each dish, highlighting their health benefits to promote healthy eating habits among consumers.

- ✓ **Celebrity Partnerships:** Celebrity mixologists or chefs should be invited to become partners of F&B brands, leveraging their expertise to elevate the quality and technique of culinary experiences.

- ✓ **Natural Ingredients:** Mixologists should prioritize using Indian ingredients and natural alternatives, reducing reliance on sugar-based syrups to create healthier beverage options.

- ✓ **Healthy Choices:** Menus should offer healthy alternatives for every food item, ensuring customers have options that prioritize their well-being.

- ✓ **Government Intervention:** The government should consider reducing GST on sugar-free drinks and implement stringent regulations requiring clear disclosure of sugar levels on packaging.

- ✓ **Labeling Transparency:** Eliminate misleading names of sugar from labeling to provide consumers with accurate information about sugar content in drinks.

- ✓ **Regulated Hours:** Late-night operations for bars and clubs should be restricted to weekends only, promoting discipline and curbing excessive drinking.

✓ **Underage Restrictions:** Strict measures should be in place to prevent underage entry into bars and clubs, with severe consequences for establishments found serving minors.

✓ **Sugar-Free Options:** Menus should include sugar-free dessert options to cater to customers seeking healthier alternatives.

✓ **Promotion of Health Brands:** Food courts and malls should actively promote health-focused brands, offering customers with diverse and nutritious dining choices.

✓ **Smoking Regulations:** Smoking should be prohibited in public areas to reduce passive smoking, with designated smoking zones or rooms provided for smokers.

✓ **Drug Policies:** Strict actions should be taken against drug usage in F&B establishments to maintain a safe and healthy environment for customers and staff.

✓ **Limiting Alcohol Serving:** Implement regulations to restrict the serving of alcohol beyond a certain limit per customer, discouraging excessive drinking and promoting responsible consumption.

✓ **Sugar-Free Cocktails:** Sugar-free cocktails should be a standard section on bar menus, providing customers with healthier beverage options.

✓ **Hygiene Standards:** Each F&B outlet should undergo regular audits to ensure proper hygiene standards are maintained, safeguarding the health of consumers.

13

Taxation and Support to Home Grown Brands

"The sanctity of law can be maintained only so as long as it is the expression of the will of the people".
– Bhagat Singh, Indian Revolutionary

The introduction of GST has imposed significant pressure on the margins of the F&B industry. Despite promising growth in GST collections and an increased coverage ratio for GST payers, the industry still struggles with the absence of input tax credit on GST and VAT. This results in higher menu prices, reflecting the elevated costs of raw materials.

The taxation system in the liquor industry is notably complex, deterring new homegrown players from entering the liquor and craft beer segments. Despite the remarkable growth of the craft beer sector, particularly in areas like Gurugram (Gurgaon) and Bengaluru (Bangalore), where summer liquor sales predominantly favor craft breweries, India has yet to witness the same home brewing revolution seen in the USA. Challenges such as attracting talent from abroad to drive innovation and creative blends hinder the growth potential of craft breweries. Furthermore, breweries in areas like Sector

29 in Gurugram (Gurgaon) often compete primarily on pricing, offering massive discounts and promotions with less emphasis on beer quality. Additionally, the high license fees and duties, coupled with restrictions on inter-state exports, confine craft breweries to single-location operations, preventing them from scaling up into larger brands.

The liquor market is largely dominated by multinational giants such as Pernod, Diageo, and AB InBev, while major players in the beer market leave little room for smaller players to flourish due to their substantial marketing and advertisement budgets. However, the surge in homegrown gin brands has prompted larger players to invest in or acquire these brands, although the underlying motivations behind such actions are often met with suspicion, as MNCs may exert dominant influence over the creative founders of these brands.

In metropolitan cities, fine dining establishments are thriving, but the average cost of dining out, especially when coupled with alcohol, exceeds Rs. 2000 per person. With additional taxes such as a 20% VAT on alcohol and a 5% GST on food, along with service charges, dining out has become increasingly costly. Obtaining permits and licenses poses another challenge for the restaurant industry, often requiring substantial payouts to intermediaries without guaranteed results.

The growth of dining and nightlife venues is largely driven by social media hype, resulting in low consumer loyalty and shorter lifespans for lounges and pubs. Rising costs have led people to opt for pre-drinks or casual gatherings over formal dining experiences. The relative affordability of MNC QSRs has further eroded the market share of lounges and clubs, prompting them to seek growth through franchising in smaller towns, creating an unstable environment in metropolitan cities with high brand turnover rates.

Homegrown QSR brands are gaining traction and challenging leading MNC QSRs in certain F&B segments. They are leveraging technology, stylish interiors, and localized menus to compete, but many rely on funding from institutions, venture capitalists, or angel investors. While these brands experience double-digit growth in store count and revenue, their losses also escalate, necessitating continuous fundraising efforts. In contrast, MNC-operated QSRs, such as the Starbucks-Tata joint venture, are on a more sustainable financial trajectory, with profitability forecasts driven by operational efficiency improvements.

Despite slower same store sales growth and expansion in aggregator offering, MNC QSR are still aggressively expanding their footprint with Jubilant Foodworks (Dominos, Hong's Kitchen, Popeyes), Burger King, Devyani International (Costa Coffee, Pizza Hut,KFC) taking the lead.

Indian QSRs must focus on offering lower-priced products and embracing technology to enhance operational efficiency. Some brands masquerading under foreign names have achieved better profitability, capitalizing on the perception that foreign brands offer better value for money.

❘ SUGGESTIONS ❘

Here are some proposed solutions to address the challenges faced by the F&B industry:

✓ **Experience over Discounts:** Shift the focus from price discounting to providing a memorable dining experience. Emphasize the quality of service, ambiance, and unique offerings to attract and retain customers.

✓ **GST Reforms:** Advocate for GST reforms by the government to enable input tax credit for the F&B industry. This would help alleviate the financial burden on businesses and potentially lead to reduced menu prices for consumers.

✓ **Technology and Customer Experience:** Homegrown QSR should prioritize leveraging technology to enhance customer experience. Invest in innovations such as mobile ordering, contactless payments, and personalized loyalty programs to improve operational efficiency and customer satisfaction.

✓ **Affordability Initiatives:** Explore strategies to make dining out more affordable for consumers. This could involve reducing portion sizes, offering simpler food options at lower price points, or focusing on creative and value-driven menu items that appeal to a wide range of budgets.

✓ **Balanced Growth:** Strike a balance between expansion and profitability. While growth is important for scaling the business, it should not come at the expense of sustainable profitability. Evaluate expansion opportunities carefully and prioritize initiatives that contribute positively to the bottom line.

Implementing these solutions could help address some of the key challenges faced by the F&B industry, fostering a more sustainable and vibrant ecosystem for businesses and consumers alike.

14

The New Age of Superfoods

"There is no hype in the dairy and superfoods industry, rather it is underpenetrated, with huge potential on the upside".
– Amit Sharma, Founder NutriMoo

The culinary landscape is rapidly evolving alongside a growing trend of lifestyle disorders emerging in people in their mid-30s. People are shifting towards superfoods and disciplined workout routines. Over the past years, many businesswomen have transitioned to pursue hobbies and prioritize social well-being apart from their homemaking roles. Often inspired by social media and the recognition garnered from viral content, these women increasingly focuses on maintaining their health through structured eating and exercise regimens, while embracing fashion and imported makeup as part of their physical transformations.

Superfoods play a pivotal role in promoting health by aiding in the reduction of high blood pressure, heart disease, diabetes, and certain cancers. These nutrient-dense foods are primarily plant-based which include berries, leafy greens, nuts, whole grains, legumes, seeds, and a variety of other items such as mushrooms, avocado, ginger, and modern liquid offerings like gut tonics, kefir, probiotics, and green tea.

My own exposure to superfoods began through a close restaurateur friend who introduced me to homemade gut tonic during a period when I was experiencing significant liver discomfort. This friend, the wife of a prominent businessman residing in Delhi's upscale NCR area, initially delivered the tonic to my home for two months as a gesture of kindness. Eventually, she realized her passion could evolve into a business venture. Subsequently, as I delved deeper into superfoods and their benefits for conditions like diabetes and fatty liver, I began noticing numerous Facebook ads for new startups addressing such health issues. Notably, brands such as Kombucha and kefir, which offer probiotics derived from milk or tea fermentation to aid digestion, have gained prominence within the superfood sector.

A multitude of startups are aggressively addressing lifestyle disorders, with more people opting for early dinners, early mornings, reduced alcohol consumption, elimination of junk food, quit smoking and prioritizing gym workouts. Following Kishore Biyani's (the Father of Retail) brands' bankruptcy due to mounting debt and the impacts of COVID-19, his daughters Ashni and Avni Biyani are making a personal comeback with 'Food Stories'. This new brand made its debut in the upscale ambiance of Delhi's Ambience Mall in *Vasant Kunj*, drawing attention for its creative approach and commitment to retail, much like their father.

Curiosity led me to explore what differentiated their new venture, especially after hearing positive social media feedback about their creativity and retail passion. Upon locating the store after a thorough search, I was surprised to find it tucked away in a quiet corner of Ambience Mall's deserted basement level, devoid of prominent branding. Despite this, I was impressed upon entering by the striking display of exotic fruits, fresh plant-based herbs, and an extensive array of seeds, nuts, and other nutritious foods—all catering to a simple underlying theme of health, superfoods, and plant-based nutrition. The upscale café within offered exclusively healthy beverages. While some imported fruits and vegetables were priced exorbitantly due to their high quality, I found myself repeatedly reminding my excited daughter to check prices before adding items to our basket. The store exuded an aura of luxury and sophistication, appealing primarily to affluent clientele.

Exiting the store, I observed two middle-aged women casually seated on golf carts with several bags, accompanied by a porter, quietly making their way towards the mall entrance. It suddenly became clear why such a service, previously unheard of in the mall's 20-year history, was available exclusively for this store.

The shift towards wellness programs and centers offering treatments like AOP, Cryo T Shocks, transformers, and Ayurvedic massages is gaining momentum. These centers often sell high-priced packages promising to reduce visceral fat and offer quick solutions for lowering body fat percentages. Wellness resorts are consistently booked during peak seasons, with some even transforming into wellness spas to capitalize on the growing demand from tourists and affluent families.

While the packaging industry for superfoods is expanding rapidly, smaller brands are leveraging marketplaces and social media ads to gain traction. Conversely, the hospitality industry, including hotels and bars, is lagging behind in adapting to these changing consumer preferences. While some brands have introduced healthy options on their menus, the launch of health-focused brands or cafes remains a largely untapped market. In comparison, destinations like Dubai and South Asian countries offer numerous superfood-based concepts, with even regular cafes providing detailed nutritional information on ingredients and cooking methods—promoting guilt-free indulgence and consumer satisfaction.

The COVID-19 pandemic initially triggered a shift towards health-conscious mindsets, prompting individuals to re-evaluate longevity and prioritize habits that enhance well-being. In the beverage sector, demand for healthier alternatives at large social events has increased notably. Despite the challenge of balancing sweetness and acidity in cocktails, the industry has yet to adopt alternatives for sweetening agents or incorporate superfoods into their offerings. A recent trend in the beverage industry involves the clarification of cocktails, a complex process promoted as a healthier and lighter alternative.

As consumer demand for healthier options continues to rise, it is imperative for industries to adapt and innovate accordingly.

There is a significant opportunity to address the issue of reverse brain drain in the food and beverage service sector. Our country possesses immense potential to educate and capitalize on the benefits of mindful, healthy living.

Startup Watch

FoodHak, a UK-based meal delivery service, specializes in nutritious yet delicious ready-to-eat meals packaged in brown pouches. They predominantly offer two packages: a weight loss program and a longevity program, both rooted in principles of plant-based nutrition, gut health reset, ayurvedic practices, and some gluten-free options. Utilizing AI-driven technology, FoodHak identifies research papers that highlight effective methods for weight management and longevity enhancement. The startup has garnered a dedicated following among foreigners and the Indian community in London. Founded by Sakshi Chhabra Mittal, who resides in London with her husband Kavin Mittal, twin son of Sunil Bharti Mittal (Chairman of Bharti Airtel Group), FoodHak addresses a growing demand for health-conscious meal solutions in urban settings.

❙ SUGGESTIONS ❙

- ✓ There is a need to integrate superfoods into Hotel Management college curricula.

- ✓ More restaurants should incorporate healthy food options seperately in their menu as these can be made delicious by refining recipes.

- ✓ Encourage and educate more chefs and bartenders to promote healthy drinks and food, and to develop special menu items that resonate with customers' health preferences.

- ✓ Facilitate collaboration between the Indian community working in the F&B industry abroad and industry leaders in India, fostering joint ventures or collaborative projects that attract them back to India by offering income opportunities comparable to US.

- ✓ Implement enhanced training and development programs for staff focusing on hygiene, advanced cooking methods, and the use of fresh ingredients. Consider highlighting and offering healthier options such as olive oil in cooking, potentially at a higher price point, to provide clients with a choice for healthier dining.

15

The Rise of Hospitality Sector in Dubai: A Case Study

"A true leader is one who creates a favorable environment
to bring out the energy and ability of his team.
A great leader creates more great leaders, and does
not reduce the institution to a single person".
– Mohammed bin Rashid Al Maktoum, Flashes of Thought

Dubai has positioned itself as a leading global tourism hub, attracting over fifteen million visitors annually with expectations to reach 25-30 million in the next 5-10 years. Renowned for its innovation, Dubai showcases top global brands in the food and beverage industry. The city hosts a diverse array of luxurious restaurant and café chains, catering to a wide range of international tourists who demand varied cuisines and top-quality service. During Dubai's scorching summers, reservations are essential for bar and nightclubs, where couples typically spend approximately INR 12,000-15,000 per outing without hesitation. The city's hospitality sector maintains standards that meet global benchmarks which reflects in the quality of drinks and culinary talent behind each brand.

Dubai's downtown, malls, and office areas buzz with prestigious international F&B chains and luxury brands. The hospitality industry has rebounded significantly post-

COVID-19, buoyed by governmental initiatives attracting top talent worldwide. Each segment of the hospitality workforce in Dubai is finely profiled to leverage unique strengths: from Asian countries like Pakistan and India dominating in construction roles, to African staff excelling in security, with Eastern Europeans and Chinese showcasing strong interpersonal skills in customer-attending roles.

Ownership of real estate in Dubai is largely held by government entities like *Nakeel* and *Emaar*, supporting grand-scale projects that attract leading global hotel chains and F&B brands. Management tie-up with these chains that enables them to tap into Dubai's burgeoning tourist market with minimal investment, driving their global presence.

Despite a substantial increase in hotel inventory, occupancy rates remain high, prompting discussions about long-term sustainability. The UAE government actively promotes tourism through global campaigns and hosts prominent events such as the Dubai Shopping Festival and World Expo to sustain year-round tourist influx. The city's infrastructure is meticulously planned, ensuring each area caters efficiently to its demographic.

Dubai's appeal extends to renowned chefs like *Ranveer Brar* and *Ritu Dalmia*, who have chosen to establish restaurants in the city over their native India, drawn by the opportunity to serve both the local community and a growing expatriate population. The presence of Michelin-starred restaurants and high compensation packages for staff underscore Dubai's allure as a global culinary destination.

In conclusion, Dubai's hospitality sector exemplifies structured growth and specialization, bolstered by strategic government support and a diverse, talented workforce. The city continues to attract top-tier talent and investment, cementing its status as a global leader in tourism and hospitality.

❘ SUGGESTIONS ❘

- ✓ Encourage expat talent to relocate to India by offering a challenging yet supportive environment with significant job responsibility and accountability.

- ✓ Implement technology-driven CRM and ERP systems for restaurant reservations. Software solutions like SevenRooms and FineDine dominate restaurant reservation systems in Dubai, while India relies heavily on a single player, limiting innovation and automation opportunities for businesses.

- ✓ Foster collaboration between hospitality associations and the India Tourism Board to launch initiatives aimed at enhancing the country's tourism ecosystem. The growth of the hospitality sector is closely tied to the overall tourism industry.

- ✓ Emphasize customer loyalty and service delivery. Fine dining establishments should prioritize in-house dining experiences over fulfilling online orders to maintain their market prestige.

- ✓ Enhance customer service through rigorous attention to hygiene standards, uniform professionalism, ongoing staff training, and impeccable presentation skills among serving staff.

- ✓ Utilize technology to automate business operations and rigorously monitor profitability to pinpoint areas of leakage and pilferage.

16

The Rise of QSR and FMCG Brands: Mobilization of Funds

"The fundamental model of our business is that in mature markets we should make profits and they shouldn't need any more outside money to grow".
– Deepinder Goyal, Founder - Zomato

The last 10 years has seen numerous homegrown brands emerging from every corner of the country, most of the pedigree of these brands has been wither product of reverse brain drain or IIT/IIM pedigree which have got lured by the influx of huge fund raising among startup and achieving the status of Unicorn. Most of the startups are working in highly competitive market with rare value proposition; thus depends on heavy marketing and advertising to stand out from the market. QSR Chains are lured by tech enabled startups like Zomato and Swiggy which spend heavy on marketing (higher marketing means higher visibility to customer) with deep discounting and packaging cost to differentiate in the market. Zomato has build an algorithm to higher visibility by giving either higher marketing cost, more deep discounting or freebies or better packaging or less turnaround time which are factors to lower profitability for the QSR outlets. Homegrown QSRs are getting energized by rapid growth of MNC QSRs which are backed by fund houses, in order to mirror their expansion, the homegrowns are getting scamper to chasing fund raising activities by venture capitalist, angel investor or foreign fund houses to build their war chest. The investors are pushing these homegrown brands to invest heavily on marketing and expansion without understanding the unit economics of the business. The fund houses which have exposure in foreign markets where larger brands are build on leveraging technology and scaling up business in profitable way , these same fund houses are pushing promoters to invest in marketing. The promoters are lost in finding new real estate, new marketing strategies and cost optimization and focusing less on ground realities. At the end of the year, the funded home grown brands after drawing their financial position have shown great revenue growth but the lack of effective cost cutting adversely impacted on the margin and profitability. Most funded homegrown brands are bleeding heavily and somewhere the total revenue is giving a good competition to net loss for the year. That means for each rupee of revenue, the company has to spend a rupee.

This has lead to promoters and fund houses scrambling for more investor to build war chest to increase runway life of the startup without pushing for single focus on profitability. The fund houses in order to give justice for their investment to their investor pool justify higher valuation based on higher revenue without looking at the loss. In most of the cases, the promoter and fund houses are able to find new investor by smart financial engineering to justify higher valuation and induct new investor. Since promoters have limited funds to reinvest in their business or have any dividend income or any clauses to cash out on their promoters, year after year they are diluting their promoter holding without realizing they are giving away a major chunk of their baby or brand to a outside investor to take over. The promoter are under the disguise that they are distributing their holding to a large pool of investor and hence they are safeguards but not realizing that all fund houses have a common of investor or have the same agenda for which they are working for : Profit! Whether they are QSR cafe brands or FMCG brands in beverages, energy drinks or packaged food, there is a similar pattern emerging in all the homegrown startup brands funded by investor.

- ✓ More than double digit of revenue growth over time
- ✓ Consistent loss-making track record
- ✓ Under 20 percent promoter holding
- ✓ 3-4 large investor dominating the board with other marginal investors pool
- ✓ Heavy investment on marketing and advertisement
- ✓ Pressure to show growth operating metrics like outlet opening, new offering, more cross selling
- ✓ Celebrities' endorsement and influencer marketing
- ✓ Opting for traditional marketing instead of guerilla marketing

What we see is a disturbing trend, the result is as follows:

- ✓ Homegrown are forced to shut shop or wind-up business
- ✓ The existing investor are funding the follow on rounds at higher valuations to sustain valuation in their books and keep the ship from sinking
- ✓ Promoter are getting drained leading to reduced interest in running business or exit leading to takeover of management by fund houses
- ✓ Cost cutting and flat in revenue growth
- ✓ Legal and defamation cases against promoters due to frauds and money laundering from the business

- ✓ Raising unsecured debt on the books at higher interest rates thereby increasing lien on physical assets of the company
- ✓ Leverage of promoter holding to raise debt to fund the businesses
- ✓ Takeover of company by strategic sale to MNC brand at throw away price or merging of business with competitors

To summarize, the homegrown F&B are being forced out of being a bigger brand giving the MNC QSR or MNC F&B brands a good headway to create monopoly business in future. The instability of promoter interest and takeover of fund houses are giving opportunities for larger brands to leverage low cost loans or funds from western countries and go on shopping spree. For homegrown QSR space, some argue that some of the local brands are doing well because of inability of MNC brands to localize their products to the taste and preference of the Indian consumer. However, MNC QSR is getting aggressive to change or tweak their menu to local taste at an affordable price point to give homegrown brands a run for their money.

❡ SUGGESTIONS ❡

- ✓ Homegrown brands should discard the traditional marketing methods and instead focus on guerilla or creative marketing strategies to gain prospective consumer mindshare.

- ✓ Startups should prefer to look at bootstrapping with friends & family money, consider raising debt or internal accruals to fund their growth.

- ✓ Brands should be their Product Market Fit (PMF) before making significant investment in marketing or advertisement for their products.

- ✓ Brands should work extensively on their unit economics of the business and before expanding their presence or outlets outside their comfort zones.

- ✓ Some of the largest brands in the world are build over a sustainable long period of time. Focus on hyper growth at initial period of time should be avoided at the cost of expense of traditional marketing and advertisement.

- ✓ Before raising funds from external investor, don't dilute more than 20 percent of your capital and keep the entire key decision making in your hand. If the business is not profitable after burning the initial capital, rethink the business model or marketing strategy.

17

Consistency + Culture + Systems + Retention = Profitable Success

*"Teamwork is the fuel that allows common people
to attain uncommon results."*
– Andrew Carnegie

During the Covid waves, Our *Chai lelo* was the only QSR brand in India which converted their entire kitchen into seva kitchen during the second wave of Covid pandemic and delivered over 25000 meals in 45 days across Delhi to Covid affected people. Our team worked harder during the pandemic to serve everyone home cooked style food. This fame brought us lot of donation from across the world to help the needy people through our initiative. We worked 24x7 and got countless calls day and night to help them deliver food to their doorstep. We delivered home cooked food to lot of Covid suffered celebrities like *Shibani Kashyap* and *Kiran Bedi* elderly couple who did not have domestic help to them serve food. We got featured in various social media platforms and WhatsApp group as a savior.

The food delivered might be average in taste but what we really delivered was the experience of getting a good meal with a click on their phone. Topped by the features like 'Meal box preference', a brown bag with disposal containers of home cooked meal was delivered within 30 minutes. Customers were able to order all three meals of the day and even the evening snack with us for a subsidized weekly subscription. This helped us grew everyday as we were consistent with our delivery and the food quality. We did this with a smile and by greeting the customers for each meal.

There have been numerous advocating statements by industry leaders about opening a restaurant or bar. They state that opening is simple but maintaining the same consistency of customer experience after a year or so is ten times more difficult. Data has shown that in western countries, a restaurant without a consistent amazing experience had a customer retention rate of around 25 percent which is quite less than a restaurant which maintained the consistency, had a retention ratio of over 70 percent. Service is a business transaction but hospitality is a personal experience. Most of the billion-dollar food service companies give credit to hospitality by delivering proper training through a systematic approach. Statistically, repeat customer spend 67 percent more.

For any successful and profitable restaurant, it is important to map out the experience which will be delivered to the customer from the moment they walk in the door until the moment they leave. Staff members should know their role in creating a good customer experience, with a proper training of what they have to deliver and how to coordinate with each other in every way is important for a successful teamwork.

"It takes 20 years to build a reputation and five minutes to ruin it. If you think about that, you'll do things differently."
– Warren Buffett

The celebrity chef *Manish Mehrotra,* the man behind 'Indian Accent' recently said in an interview that a good service can hide bad food but if good food not served well can destroy the brand. *Manish* is an example of a reverse brain drain that was brought back to India in 2009 by *Rohit Khattar* to run the Indian Accent at the Manor. Indian Accent is a perfect example, how a chef was given ownership to run the brand with relentless focus on good food and service made it the only Indian brand to be featured in Asia's 50 Best Restaurants. When you have consistency, people know what they are going to get and that helps build the foundation for a successful restaurant.

One of the key traits of a success is great culture which is built by great leadership. Most of the times, issues arises when managers act like bosses, indulging in power trips and creating toxicity in work environment.

> *"Motivate them, train them, care about them, and make*
> *winners out of them… they'll treat the customers right.*
> *And if customers are treated right, they'll come back."*
> — *J. Willard Marriott, founder of the Marriott Corporation*

Creating a strong culture is a continuous process which requires effort from each member of staff. One of the biggest lag in the Indian hospitality industry has been the lack of training. Training is everything. Training is not always about how to make food and beverage. It is a vast subject which would cover the intent of running the establishment – the mission statement, the core value and the story behind why you opened the restaurant. Share your passion. Every new team member should get training from day one so it sets the tone for excellence from day one.

Creating systems is the spinal cord for any restaurant. Systems should be strong enough and upscale to be efficient for the staff and the effort goes in managing the system and not employees.

Lastly, train your staff to be salesperson for your brand. They are selling an experience, perceived value and a reason for the customer to visit again. Word of mouth can create wonders for a brand.

❙ SUGGESTIONS ❙

- ✓ Lead, inspire and motivate your staff for continuous improvement, provide opportunity for growth, celebrate achievement and encourage ownership to create great culture

- ✓ Assess current challenges, set clear goals and expectation, implement and train managers for advance leadership training, establish systems and accountability, create a culture of continuous improvement and providing tools for success

- ✓ Every restaurant should have a short manual which covers food and drink description, hospitality experience, steps of service and how to get a win with the customer

- ✓ Conduct regular staff meetings discussing shift expectation, spot quizzing, sharing any wins, staff feedback. Avoid holding separate team meetings; all staff should be present together so everyone is on the same page.

- ✓ System to run the restaurant has to be thoroughly planned, discussed with management and each staff has to be tracked to the system so that they stay motivated to follow and deliver consistent experience for the customer

- ✓ Provide comprehensive selling training session which includes verbal skills, building rapport and trust with customer, creating upsell opportunities, handling objections and complaints.

18

Guerrilla Marketing Case Studies

What is Guerrilla Marketing?

Invented in 1984 by advertising executive 'Jay Conrad Levinson', guerrilla marketing signified a shift from traditional media (print, television, and radio) to digital and viral marketing.

Guerrilla Marketing is an advertising strategy that employs unconventional mechanisms that helps to promote particular product or service in a cost-effective way.

It lay emphasis on creativity with authencity to attract customer's attention. This approach often involves Street Marketing, Viral Marketing, Experiential Marketing, Free Samples etc. alongwith other marketing methods which aims to generate buzz and promotion without burning large amount of funds. Guerrilla Marketing relies more on creativity and innovative methods than on large investments.

The ultimate goal is to create a memorable experience which encourages the customer to interact with the brand and share their experiences with others, leading to word-of-mouth promotion.

Some of the biggest guerilla marketing are:

1. Burger King's Moldy Whopper

In an unexpected move in the history of fast food advertising, Burger King showcased a time-lapse video featuring a decaying Whopper burger over 35 days. This campaign aimed to highlight their success in eliminating artificial preservatives from the Whopper sandwich in European countries and the United States. Despite the initially unsettling visuals of mold growing on the burger, the advertisement effectively conveyed its message with a caption referencing the absence of artificial preservatives. Surprisingly, the unconventional approach resonated positively with the target audience, sparking interest and even preference for the Whopper burger over competitors.

2. | Airbnb's 'Night At' Campaign

Airbnb's experiential marketing campaign "Night At" made headlines by transforming iconic locations into exclusive accommodations. Starting with 'the Louvre' Museum's glass pyramid, where guests could sleep surrounded by priceless artworks like the Mona Lisa, Airbnb bridged art and hospitality, creating lasting impressions for art enthusiasts.

Expanding beyond Airbnb offered unique stays at diverse venues such as the Shark Aquarium, the Paris catacombs (timed for Halloween), Dracula's Castle in Transylvania, and the Great Barrier Reef. Each location provided an immersive experience, allowing guests to connect deeply with cultural, emotional, and historical significance.

3. | UNICEF's Vending Machine

UNICEF initiated a guerilla marketing campaign in 2009 to raise awareness about the global issue of contaminated water, which claims over 4000 lives daily. In New York's Union Square, they installed a provocative "Dirty Water Vending Machine." This machine offered bottles of visibly dirty water labeled with diseases such as malaria, typhoid, and cholera, highlighting the harsh reality faced by communities lacking access to clean drinking water.

For a $1 donation to UNICEF, participants could obtain a bottle of brown, unfiltered water containing visible particles. UNICEF emphasized that each $1 donation could provide a child with clean drinking water for approximately 40 days, underscoring the impact of their cause.

This campaign aimed not only to raise awareness but also to prompt tangible support for UNICEF's efforts to alleviate the global water crisis.

4. | Break Me if You Can - 3M Security Glass

The 3M Security Glass guerrilla marketing campaign became legendary when $3 million was encased in what was presented as 3M's 'bulletproof' glass. Passers-by were invited by a uniformed security guard to attempt to break the glass using only their feet. The incentive: anyone successful would keep the $3 million. However, unbeknownst to participants, almost all of the money was fake, except for $500 on the top layer. The glass was not bulletproof but was indeed designed to withstand kicks.

Only a select few individuals were allowed to attempt to break the glass, yet despite this limited participation, the image and story of the campaign were shared millions of times worldwide.

5. "Share a Coke" Campaign

One of Coca-Cola's standout guerrilla marketing successes was the "Share a Coke" campaign. This initiative encouraged customers to search for Coke bottles personalized with their own names or those of friends and family, and share photos with these bottles on social media. By prompting engagement through personalization, the campaign significantly boosted Coca-Cola's brand visibility. Moreover, it drove sales as customers purchased multiple bottles to collect all the different names available. The campaign proved effective in both strengthening brand connection and driving consumer interaction.

Epilogue

I resigned from my highly lucrative investment banking job on October 4, 2015, the same day my beautiful daughter was born. Her age serves as both a reminder and a barometer of my entrepreneurial journey. Despite navigating numerous jobs and degrees since my days at Modern School, Vasant Vihar, transitioning to an uncharted industry felt nerve-wracking yet exhilarating. I embarked on something with no clear direction, unsure of what I aimed to achieve.

As I pivoted into the hospitality industry, I gradually realized that my greatest asset was empathy, a trait inherited from my mother, who tragically passed away at 52 due to complications from severe diabetes. Her loss deeply affected my mental stability, leading to severe anxiety and depression at a young age of 27. Immersing myself in business became a potent escape, consuming up to 18 hours a day and temporarily erasing negative thoughts.

In the initial years, while developing the concept of Cocktail Week from 2015 to 2017, I invested extensive hours, often up to 18 hours daily. Though I felt a sense of achievement, my newness to the industry and reliance on blind trust left me struggling, with uncertain prospects of sustaining my presence. Yet, guided by an unseen force, I persisted, exploring new avenues to establish a viable business.

In May 2022, I experienced a mental wellness program led by Ramon Lamba, whom my wife discovered through a reference. Interestingly, I had organized a cocktail bar for her son's wedding in Goa a year earlier. Impressed by our work, her daughter-in-law invited us to a 7-day wellness retreat in Goa, focusing on manifestation, breathing exercises, meditation, overcoming fears, and clearing mental clutter. This experience provided clarity and redirected my energies toward meaningful pursuits. It allowed me to delve into our inner beliefs and discover our true calling, empowering us to make a significant impact.

In our entrepreneurial journey, there were moments of despair and betrayal, yet resilience and patience revealed that greater plans were in store. When you engage in impactful endeavors with genuine intentions, opportunities align, connecting dots toward a purposeful life.

Over the past decade, I have become emotionally invested in numerous brands and bartenders. Recognizing my role and that of my team in guiding this industry, I've assumed internal leadership to shape a framework for improvement across our various company brands. As the old proverb, , goes, "With great power comes great responsibility."

This book serves to crystallize my thoughts, identify pain points, and propose solutions. Importantly, it aims to address industry challenges positively and collectively transform our sector from merely surviving to thriving. While I may not have had all the answers or direction back in 2015, I am certain that our collective efforts can inspire and empower lives within this industry. Witnessing many individuals grow into independent, successful leaders over the past decade brings me immense joy. Small opportunities provided to them have transformed their lives significantly. Imagine expanding this infrastructure and collaborating to uplift more people.

In a country of over 1.4 billion people, with high unemployment in rural areas, the hospitality industry presents an opportunity to bridge gaps, upskill individuals, and integrate them into a burgeoning sector. It is imperative to cultivate an organized, supportive, and positive industry mindset, working collaboratively toward common goals.

Through our initiatives, we are establishing a robust ecosystem within the hospitality industry over the next five years to address these challenges. We recently launched the IBG Bar Academy, focusing on upskilling talent from underprivileged backgrounds in small towns through digital platforms, followed by job placements in leading F&B brands. Additionally, we are enhancing the India Bartenders Guild to serve as a pinnacle association for bartenders in India, offering bar licenses and knowledge through masterclasses and trainer guidance.

Looking ahead, we plan to organize inter-IHM college competitions, offering new students a fresh perspective on beverages. These colleges traditionally leave students with limited job prospects, often relegated to menial roles within hotels. We are introducing the IBG-endorsed Professional Bartenders Book across 250+ IHM colleges through academic partnerships. Furthermore, we are advocating with the International Bartenders Association (IBA) for India's permanent membership, enabling our talent to compete globally in the World Cocktail Competition and facilitating knowledge exchange among member associations.

Through Elixir Coterie Bar Consulting, we are collaborating with restaurants and bars to optimize their beverage menus for profitability. Additionally, we support new liquor brands lacking substantial marketing budgets by facilitating access to bars and enhancing awareness among our bartender community through training and masterclasses.

Elixir Bar Solutions, specializing in setting up bars at social events and weddings, is committed to developing no-sugar or low-sugar beverage menus. We promote fresh juices and smoothies, elevating beverage experiences at events. With operations launched in Dubai, we are sourcing global talent and raw materials to enhance beverage service quality in India, addressing past challenges related to ingredient supply.

I would like to end this with my favorite quote which has guided me from last 15 years.

> *'Live as if you were to die tomorrow.*
> *Learn as if you were to live forever.'*
> – *Mahatma Gandhi*

❑❑❑

About the Author

Archit's journey unfolds from the world of finance to the realm of hospitality, marking a significant transition that has defined his remarkable trajectory. Armed with a B.Com (Hons), MBA in Finance and Business Management from IIM Lucknow, and a CFA charter, he has mastered the numbers game. However, Archit's narrative takes an exciting turn as he emerges as the creative force behind over 10 hospitality brands, including Cocktail Week, Beer Week, Elixir Bar Solutions, To the Teaz, Chai Lelo, and the India Bartender's Guild.

Recognized with the 2021 Economic Times Inspiring Leaders Award for North India, Archit's fusion of finance and hospitality embodies innovation and success. He currently serves as the President of India's Bartender's Guild and has successfully facilitated India's membership in the International Bartender Association. Recently, he established the IBG Bar Academy, aiming to provide training and mentorship to aspiring bartenders from underprivileged backgrounds, thereby striving to elevate bartending to a respected profession with equitable pay and standardized certification programs.

Before entering the hospitality industry, Archit garnered over 6 years of experience in investment banking with firms like E&Y, BDO, Escort Mutual Fund, and Prabhudas Lilladher, specializing in market research, valuation, and investment management. He is married and blessed with a daughter, balancing his professional achievements with personal fulfillment.

✉ architsinghal86@gmail.com

 @elixirbarsolutions @cocktailweekindia
@chaileloindia @indiabartendersguild
@ibgbaracademy @totheteaz
@beerweekindia @culinaryexperienceindia
@indiapubcrawl @thecocktailshopindia

❑❑❑